Numb and Number

By the same author:

Poetry
To Thalia
On Reflection
Watermark
Open Water (audio CD)
Phantom Limb
Concrete Tuesday
Anatomy of Voice
New & Selected Poems
Mishearing

Fiction
Glissando: A Melodrama

Non-Fiction
Grotesque Anatomies: Menippean Satire Since the Renaissance
Feeding the Ghost 1: Criticism on Contemporary Australian Poetry
(edited with Andy Kissane and Carolyn Rickett)

Anthology
Contemporary Australian Poetry (edited with Martin Langford,
Judith Beveridge and Judy Johnson)

Numb and Number

David Musgrave

PUNCHER & WATTMANN

First published in 2019

Published by Puncher & Wattmann
PO Box 279
Waratah NSW 2298

http://www.puncherandwattmann.com
puncherandwattmann@bigpond.com

ISBN 9781925780383

NATIONAL
LIBRARY
OF AUSTRALIA

A catalogue record for this book is available from the National Library of Australia

Printed by Lightning Source International

Cover photograph: Phillip Musgrave

Cover design by Miranda Douglas

给琴

Contents

1

Coastline

I walked along the cliff-top at around eleven
one September morning, wondering why the level
of the sea at the horizon
seems always higher than where I am, even though
the waves kept shuddering into spray on rocks far below.

Was it a kind of horizontal vertigo,
or a species of the sublime, a newly released *cogito*,
I think therefore… I must be a dwarf
standing on the shoulders of other dwarves, each one shorter
than the one before? I filed this thought for

later use and kept walking past clumps of hustling
grass, on a concrete path glittering in bright sunlight,
past a jogger threshing air,
all elbows, knees and sweat, who paused a moment, oinked,
or so it seemed, and jogged on. The morning light coined

a mint of silver on the ocean, golden shivers
of droughty stalks flared from the footpath's fissures
and I was rich for a moment,
richer than the waterfront exclusionary
viewkeepers, the prinked promenaders, even the cemetery.

I passed a clique of tourists gathered at a corner
of the white retaining fence, where locals reckon
the face of the Virgin Mary
appears each day at around eleven, and armed with cameras
and mobile phones they waited with a calm air as

if faith was merely a matter of patience. I prepared
to wait for a while as well, but nothing appeared
to happen, so I strolled on, dissatisfied
as ever. Back then I wanted to be an anagram
of what I should have been: not a Manager,

but a flâneur perhaps, or a traveller or taghairm
prophesying in ox-hide by a stream, or migrate
in reverse to my two great-
grandfathers, Musgrave and Quealy, who lived across the Shannon
from each other but never knew it, sang their Hosannas

to different Gods and croaked here only eighty miles
and twenty years apart. Would I assimilate
or be assimilated there,
an exile in a land of unfamiliar rain,
a thonged exotic flaw in emerald terrain?

No theme comes from exile except exile, something
no one bothered to tell the ex-pat generation.
Until now, I thought.
I watched some yachts puff south like beery slobs, all gut
and no behind. A seagull carried on like a galoot

above my head and then the path began declining
into oblongs balkanized by weed-cracks, kindling
memories of jigsaws:
fitting patiently on wet Sundays piece to piece,
sifting through the pile for the opposite

of a promontory of cloud: portly swastikas,
running men, whimsies, wheat sacks,
Swedens, Sulawesis, bits
of continent or a cauliflowered florescence, Mandelbrots
ferning into shapes running through my bloodstream.

And then the bigger pieces: the absent shape of you
to which no piece will fit, like emptied rooms
in a house no longer habitable.
Loss ineluctable: there is no cure, no magic zebra
crossing to a lossless world. Aslant in the breeze

I walked the cliff-top walk, totally alone
at the other end of love, on the way from one littoral
to another, balancing an act
in a world out of balance, piecing together words
to confront something, long ago put to the sword.

Level with my eyes a seagull hovered, motionless
into the wind. I passed beer cans in modern middens,
dandelions on the path's port side
while slowly from the north-east, thunderheads of mackerel-
mottled clouds began to coolly spit on the caramel-

coloured cliffs. It's funny how it worms
its way in, love, diasporated like a swarm
of angry bees bearing a heart.
The continents are the oldest divorcees, having drifted
apart for eons. Next to them we've barely tiffed.

But still you reappear, even if only as a pronoun
which has to be emptied out or not pronounced
as once it was: as you.
Almost anyone could be one of them,
an economy of love which we won't fathom.

You can stand for anyone now, there is no end:
the reader of this poem or the one you need
as elementally as air.
And so I kept on walking, finding in a word the future
and the past in ever-repeating series bearing a kind of fruit

into the present. And as I walked, I came to resemble Achilles
racing the tortoise, never overcoming, in the end, a calculus
of ever decreasing lengths.
But I wasn't frustrated — *au contraire* — I was fascinated:
for love, like every coastline, properly considered, is infinite.

The Manuscript

As he watched the last of the manuscript curl into ash
he followed her footsteps of years ago
past the blue metal swathe of rail,
down narrow acacia, callistemon streets
towards the silos and scrap metal merchants,
through the underpass that resembled a public urinal
with its stench, mossy drippings and gridded lights
to the bachelor flat at the rear of a house that groaned and shuddered
with each passing train, imagined as he found it to be, years later,
a gas spigot beaking one corner, a cobwebbed window looking over
a concrete backyard, little more than a bed and kitchenette
disappearing into ionised air, he realised
he'd stubbed out the last of a stubborn obsession, but not the story
of how, night after night, she'd traverse the restless suburb
then after each assignation return through the urinous underpass,
up the narrow acacia, callistemon streets to the share house
where her daughter was baby-sat, the details perduring
for decades after he'd read it, then scattered the ash in their garden
and how, decades after she'd left for the second-last last time, she'd forgotten
ever having typed it up in the desert, plotting her return.

Lines in Lviv, formerly Lvov, formerly Lemburg, near Limbo

The fine art of pretension, putting on airs
is exemplified by this, sitting in an outdoor cafe
on a chair tilting on cobblestones
watching the block-headed polity walk past,
hard starers every one of them,
cheerful and grim, indifferent to this sketching
which seems to slide easily into the sunlight
of a tree's blazing green head of hair
and the glowering sky, cool as a separation.
A clarinet, played well, breezes through the streets,
its notes as distinct and indistinct as turning inwards
once more, now the shouting in the square has died down
and the crowds are trudging back home, the earth relaxing
into its orbit once again. A dim sheen
rises now from the cobblestones as a pigeon inspects
each bump as thoroughly as a phrenologist.

It's like a giant family, being in a country
as monocultural, everyone a distant relation
except me. And that's fine.
I've examined myself in the mirror
and wouldn't dream of inflicting my relatedness
on anyone who didn't want it.
The telegraph wires are a nodal symphony
stretching across the street and sagging
into emptiness. Who wants to know about a poet
by his or her poetry? Wouldn't a blood test be easier,
or a DNA swab? Leave me out of it,
I'm just filling in time before I go.

The Project

Let's shut it down.
Let's shut down the project.
There are protocols to be disregarded,
but don't shred the paperwork.
Let's let it all happen, slowly
but not as slow as an ice age.

But if it isn't our project
can we shut it down? Sure
we can, just like folding
the news up under an arm
then tossing it into the garbage.
But I'd like to return to the project.

I think we should shut it down.
I think it has run its course.
There are only so many efficiency dividends
and property keeps on rising. Bubbles
nibble the meniscus of my beer
which is further evidence of what

needs to be done: within the message
vacuity is necessary, and vacuity
is a dark attractor. Let's keep going
and keep this in mind. A tennis ball
ages like a middle-aged man
but middle-aged men are not tennis balls

even when they hit the net
trying to prove their relevance
like flies head-butting warm windows
or the dead sea of a white page filling with fly shit.
Ordinarily, that page would have been printed on
with schedules, memos, details of the project

but this no longer concerns us.
What matters is shutting down the project.
It no longer has a cost centre, but its costs
are incalculable. Shutting it down
is neither penny wise nor pound foolish:
it's entering the cave again, eyes wide open.

The Cave

opens into a blackened roof, veined
and drying, and out of it issuing
sighs or rattles. So small, and yet
it dominates the room. Wetting now and then
with swabs does nothing to slow down
the shallowing breath, the chill creeping
in from the limbs. Through it all, her eyes
stay open, seeing everything and nothing.

The Narcolept

The dinosaurs live on in chickens
and the dreams of an old woman
beached by an ocean of palsied sleep.

She's following their footprints back
to a time before sleep, roving
behind her eyelids, her soft palate

furling and unfurling like a flag.
For as long as I can remember, I lacked
confidence in consciousness. I'd watch

for ironing burning or pry open
sleeping eyes. Now it is the empty O
of agèd sleep drawing up alongside

death in that dream of ancient traffic,
those prehistoric footprints arrowing back
toward the start of the dream. Beyond extinction.

Filing Cabinet

Kind of a coffin, it stands in my study, almost
as high and as wide. Its three drawers are shut,
flush with its front wire and paper guts
in a wooden body. I don't know quite how to fill it:
God knows I've tried almost everything: genre, alphabet,
my different selves, the money spent. To keep it
satisfied, letters, faxes, poems, and bills
are never enough: it wants to annex the kingdom
of miscellaneous, which rules from paper towers
on top of it. It must be a family thing.
My mother was taxed in her later years
by paper taking over her house,
rearranging her mind in changing piles.
I'm much the same. Poetry is what escapes the files.

Five Years Later

Seeing you today at the peace march, I could have slapped you
as you walked by and you wouldn't have seen it coming,
grey-green eyes absorbed in mournful hardness.
Charisma is a sponge
which sometimes needs wringing out.
Five years, I think, and now you're dyeing,
dressing still like twenty-somethings dress,
but thicker through the middle, calves like ninepins.
I thought I'd see a baby at your hip,
but you were alone, with another.
Compassion is less honest than intimacy.
At one with the crowd, I watched you swell
up George Street to the park
where you settled on the grass
and glittered in the heat. Then I came home.
There was no peace, or explanation:
such privacy, in public.
The sun went on trepanning the sky.

The Ash Field

1. The phone call from China

You can tell by its garden the rented house:
hardy perennials, the lawn resentfully shaved
and gutters backed up with gossip.
Nevertheless it's home, musty
in winter, a yeasty
ferment in summer.
It's hard not to remember it
as it became: emptied out,
a wardrobe's worth of shoes
left for litter. Before, the walls were lined with books,
the evenings Chinese whispers
until one of them became a squall.

2. Naked

If she could have slept, she might have dreamed of me
as I dreamed of her, or at least her absent shape.
I was in that house and there were rooms I'd never seen before
full of trappings and possessions I didn't know
belonged to her. The world came in to inspect it.
Someone gave me a veil — to wear or to escape in?
If I had been mere bones, I couldn't have been more naked.
It's because the world always already knows
and we're the ones who find out last of all.

3. Trees

The trees are full of tinnitus and light.
A fat fly walks lazily down the stem
of a vine to shade itself. The cortex
of the she-oak slowly wakes into a skink.
The morning air smells damp and burnt, skeined
with the wool of the smouldering log
still going from last night. Grey heat
glows at its edges, breathing smoke.
The she-oak is ancient and eyed with lost limbs,
the little lizards ascending and descending
like angels or truncated rivers striped with light.
The low-hanging clouds threaten a hostile takeover
of the smoke, but settle for my beard.
Is it true that a mirror decays?

4. Numb and Number

Quhilk is begun with inconstance,
And endis nocht but variance,
Scho haldis with continuance
    No serviture.
—William Dunbar, 'Inconstancy of Luve'

Which is worse: wasting years
in a labyrinth of grief, faithful
as an old boot, or brushing it off
like a cobwebbed leaf on a sleeve
or a mis-named fact?

Both will get you to where you're headed.

Take 'the phone call from China'.
Back then, I never got to see the number
but it wasn't who she said it was that deranged her:
not the suicide of a spurned lover in Singapore
or Bad Uncle, who'd shuffled off some years before,
but you, you piece of shit—I should explain:
'piece of shit' is a metaphysical term, denoting
a pigment of the imagination
which gets trekked in from the mis-remembered past
to stain the present, reminding with its stench
that there's always an outside to every intimation;
one synonym is 'carnal over-reach',
'numbness of the censors' is another—
and since we'll never speak again,
it's time to call you out, piece of shit,
as now at last I have your number:
you're the kind that has to keep on taking,
smart-arsed clerk, your family not enough,
numbing all around you without shame.

Now, you linger in my present.
Having taken what I once thought was my past, I'm glad
you leave me nothing.

I clean my shoe.

The Analyst

It's not the ziggurat
of DSMs and textbooks piled on the desk
nor the flag of surrender, waving feebly
from the adjacent box of tissues;
it's not the suggestion that any occupation
other than poet would be preferable,
financially and spiritually speaking,
nor the age difference, objectively speaking,
nor the speaking cure at which she believes she excels;
it's not the sharkskin sky
nor the gutter pattering softly as the snare
in Al Green's 'Take Me to the River';
but the way my analyst's dewlaps quiver
with all the inward pleasure
of revealing her entrancement by my ex
(apparently they haven't gotten to me yet).

Nine Crab Barn

I made my way to Nine Crab Barn
    and found there all the details of my brief:
        curate the present, facilitate, on no account
create or show signs of belief.

All the people that I loved
    were at a near remove, some near the bar,
        others at the exits talking, making jokes,
some pleased to see me, some in fear

of something they refused to see
    in me, or in themselves: the hair-trigger
        which goes off on the freeway and makes a ute
carousel in elegant figures

of eight and greet a safety rail
    like a love-tap or a peck on the cheek gone wrong.
        I didn't drive but swam as briskly as the moon
in cloud at night, partly hidden in song-

light, laughing. Nine Crab Barn —
    I'd heard the name before, a whispered spell
        incanted over whiskey or set in circus fonts
on posters in the Star Hotel

and mentioned in biographies
    of the Selfish Generation. Nine Crab Barn,
        where it all once happened, where customers still sat
savouring the Great Man's yarn

of what went on, with whom, and when,
      the mythology of proper names. I
         would say, "get fucked" to the lot of them, sycophants
and jerks and jumped-up literati

but then again, that's the problem
      I went there in the first place to address:
         the way mood shifts instantly from ecstasy to hate,
the way we fail our otherness.

Even though I'd never seen
      Nine Crab Barn before, I knew it well.
         It was capital of all the lost cost collectors
of the love-you hate-me soul.

Through the wave-crests, through the bottom
      of a schooner, through its sails, I'd
         dreamed it, through the foil-bright harbour baffling dusk
I'd dreamed it on the failing tide

of modern gentleness and hurt.
      It's where I came to learn the following home-grown
         truths: that every motorist is a satirist finding in traffic
every failing but her own;

that every day will have its dog;
      too many crooks (or is that cocks?) spoil
         the brothel. The homespun is an undecidable thing,
and means whatever you want to be real.

I arrived at Nine Crab Barn bang on midnight
      in doubting moonlight, its rooms ablaze with pleasure,
         music like a snake in flight from a jukebox yelling
into the night's black ear.

I found my room and dumped my bags
    and joined in unforgiving, blaring light
        all those others, all those I had loved and failed.
Now it is the place I write.

Fire

The only thing that travels faster than light
is its shadow: systems in eclipse
or the failure of an ancestor
hurtling out of the past to nobble a future.
Fire at a distance
is an index of love —
bright fire falling over buildings,
over heritage sandstone and embryonic gardens,
honing its shadows, the streetlight
rippling across the uneven lawn
or a truck's high beam lifting a driver's head
and punting it into darkness. Fire inside
meets fire from afar, a puddle
rises to soften the sun or a spider
springs into light, levering across its web,
and shadows onto its prey.
The fire inside you
radiates in all directions
and the shadow it casts from me
is where I have always been
but now will never go.

Beijing Dectets

reflection I

whatever words I have   come back
    as burred tokens   relief worn smooth
or sound   with a sense only partly for me
    the city   a set of controlled mirrors
shopfront   windscreen   commerce
    heavenly haze   miasma   cigarette fug
or dry dust-fog   a pedestrian tunnel under the freeway
    leads to the metro   a pony stands near the entrance
harnessed to the day   selling mulberries
    blackberries   spiral-peeled pineapples

reflection II

voluntaries of sunlight dog the river
    a vortex here   a dimpling furrow there
what's the difference   canal or paved river?
    timber-knotted currents   whorl and glitter
offering up the sky   in mosaic flow
    under the bridges   a compost of midges
a fishing line's sagging hypotenuse
    in contrapuntal flow   rival yellow
blue and orange bicycles   move midway
    above the canal   below the rumbling road

LII

In my fifty-third year towards heaven, my beard
    shot through with white, like tissue-flecked washing,
I removed myself to the Northern Capital
    to spend my days in study and contemplation
communing with nature on CCTV 2
    far from the poisoned coteries and cliques
where judgements are capricious, bitter
    and absolute as those of the ancient gods;
I prefer the problems of being alien,
    provincial and unique; a foxed mirror

question

some days the light finds me
    like a grinch   devoid of grace
the streets hemmed in haze   a bare tree
asks a question   bicycles and scooters
turning cars   the heavy sooting trucks, long buses
    give their answers   the sun is a distant wen
seeping onto buildings   easily discerned
    in white and grey   air thickens into
willow buds: heads of sparse hair
    dreaded with green   rising from tufted earth

mullock

my thinking is done in pacing   dodging
       we: islands   of sputum
a quincunx of strawberries   one corner of it squashed
       over cracked pavers   skirting mullock
which is the thinking of composition
       barrages for the human rapids
who are at home here   walking beside the calm
       canal   drooping willows   a tranny ablaze
in a paved recess   an aged couple
       ballroom dancing in the gloom

blossoming

Spring is the deeper way   than freeways
       and smog   under the hood
there are systems   and redundancies
       and for two weeks   flowers opening
plane tree fuzz   above our heads
       and in our throats   a prickling foil
such burgeoning   requires deep soil
       thick genetic rivers   perfectly muddied
with you away   this place is a delicious
       prison   such pleasure in discovering

facemask

a facemask becomes me   so that only by my eyes
          can I be known   I become a facemask
shuffled out among cities   streets lanes
          and restaurants I will know them
as the canulating veins in my wrists   knuckles
          ciliae destroyed by endless smog   know numbers
for the verities and vices   inconstant moonlight
          consumption and decay   by rectifying
the incongruity of names   lies the future
          swipe down to search   swipe left to like

tomb sweeping (qingming) I

Gēge runs the show in Tiger Hollow
          the hills behind the hamlet
where my father-in-law grew up
          his house   a cottage of one or two rooms
we are the ring-ins   me and the little boy
          on a matrilineal line   following Gēge's lead
we'll end up at the plots   the living have reserved
          later we'll eat cousin Lǐ Liúfú's organic food
bamboozled in equal measure   by the table-talk
          in sūsònghuà   and by the báijiǔ

tomb sweeping (qingming) II

tumulus by tumulus   we let off bungers
        and poured out wine   for the Lǐ family dead
burned hell banknotes for those who starved to death
        or died of old age   the grass soughs
but nothing stirs in the undergrowth
the freeway only metres away
as we kowtow to the past   the dead know more
        than we do   like where we'll be
in a century   and how the light here
        sharpens everything on time's lathe

smokescreen

spring's method is surprise:
a green glimmer mingling
smokeflowers with bloodblossoms,

dirty cool air with a hot sun.
In a couple of weeks it's over:
all the trees luxuriate in green

and the wind harvests voices
from the leaves. All this is smoke-
screen for the work it's done in you

this little nub of ours   this autumn bloom

Waratah

Then the Giant-killer handed me a herb he had plucked from the ground, and showed me what it was like. It had a black root and a milk-white flower. The gods call it Moly, and it is an awkward plant to dig up, at any rate for a mere man. But the gods, after all, can do anything.
Book X: Circe, *The Odyssey*, trans. E.V. Rieu

1.
I'm clearing a space in Waratah.
Here, in Waratah, I'm making a clearing,
marking out space among bluetongues, grevilleas,
a conurbation of ants' nests. I'm making a space
the size of a mid-range imagination,
a modest keep, a distillation of hope.
I'm chucking out, I'm ringing in, and I'm wiping clean
here in Waratah, leaving a burly wake. I'm stacking
and hanging, playing and putting away: Dada to one side,
Villa-Lobos the other, the Velvets and Cesar Vallejo,
Li Bai, *Satura*, Pantagruel feasting in Paris. Somewhere
among these, to one side, maybe just over the way
I'm clearing more spaces in Waratah. Here.

2.
There's a brawl of clouds over Kooragang.
White on grey, duck egg on magnetite, piled up high on each other,
stacking up like a freeway disaster. All day, inland heat
has been steepling, stifling the river. Up through the palms
a quiver of Chisel, magpie bubble-song, backyard breezes
outing their bounds, shouldering their way through vines,
making their way to this space I'm clearing in Waratah.
I'm growing a thousand lanterns curled in bright green shade,
chandeliers of tucked seahorse, an oast of spice
as hot as the early summer heat. I'm clearing a space for them too.

3.
George Thomas Ferris, I'm back here in Waratah.
John Blake Quealy, I'm here in my clearing.
Respectful as a body of undertakers
aloof from a family's grief, the currawongs
confer on the nature strip opposite, stepping daintily on scaly feet
or supine, receiving the beak of a mate, rampant with grey fluffy breast.
Wintergrass, buffalo, paspalum, couch niggle over the lawn,
carpet my clearing with their bladed relations.
Dorothy Downs Pawsey, I'm back here in Newcastle.
Eliza Augusta Prentice, I'm just down the road.

4.
I'm building a structure of time and air,
mortared by sound. I'm piecing it together,
here in the shadow of the Moly-Cop mastaba,
flanged by the two-carriage whistle of Maitland trains.
In the smoke-quiet streets of Waratah, you can see people
smoking moly in rollies, dealing moly in parks;
in The Town Hall, the Royal, in Waratah Park,
the hushed business of moly. Property prices
go hand in hand with molyfication. That's why the Moly-Cops
are just down the road, regulating, confiscating, keeping it all
in hand. But I'm with Gryllus on that one, I never touch the stuff.
I prefer to stay as I am, snuffling around.

5.
Across from ours, a weatherboard house
and a Woolworths shopping trolley parked on the nature strip,
Newcastle trees, angophora, turpentine, palings the colour of old bone.
A brown bluetongue suns itself. Carers of the old and dying
come and go in shifts. The steelworks shriek intermittently,
minting and banging. Threading the clangour of industry,
a long train of portbound extinction.
Mynahs attack the bluetongue; a baby currawong
shivers on the hills hoist. Hail and tar, fledgling leaves,
the scratch of lungsmoke wood-burning.

6.
I'm pitching a tent in the blue field of death.
The spring maggies swoop, spiteful
as early Mick Jagger lyrics, and just as lively.
The frangipanis peep out little green horns,
leaf-hooks and spiderwebs furtive with death.
A powerful owl monsters the baby currawong,
the mynahs shit on the roof. Lorikeets
and wattlebirds pilfer the bright red bottlebrush flower,
tweeting their restaurant reviews. Silence
is everywhere else but here, in Waratah.

7.
I'm adding my bit to the Waratah Symphony.
I'm tempering my piano, running my fingers over its keys,
good teeth and bad teeth, major and minor.
I'm tuning the strings, composing a private cantata,
savouring note after note in a climacteric
of joy. I'm painting the space I'm clearing
with low humid sounds and high nips of light.
Now, we're inkling the air with song, we're singing
here, in Waratah, a piece for love and piano
in the key of near. We're clearing a space for song.

京禧

I perform a Vulcan mind-meld on my son
who's only two weeks old, but quite receptive.
As I touch his forehead, his eyelids close
like two shelled almonds.
I see alabaster mountains
topped with porphyry, a chorus
of light and fuzzy dark,
teething curves, milky ecstasies ...
I can't tell what Jingxi sees in me: he shifts
a little uncomfortably, his brow
ridges, then he screams.

Information Theory 2

I have this little piece of information.
It weighs about eight kilograms.
Its fingers, toes are just like mine
but its consciousness of each of them isn't.

I call it 'information'. It calls me 'oo-wa'
sometimes, at other times just 'waa'.
It has a low tolerance for redundancy
and a preference for entropy.

Its skin is a pinguid resin
of amino acids, capillaries and down.
It forages in my delight
and smells like an unwashed mouse.

2

The Transportations of George Bruce

We were naked.
We watched, from the thick part of the woods,
the police take the others away. It was raining,
the depth of winter, the sky black as loss,
the trees of our camp aglow with the fire
which had warmed us. There had been five of us
untimely mortals plus our Judas, who was spared,
leaving Meredith, Farr and me. The other two hanged.

At the midnight hour I'd heard the snapping of twigs,
the stamp of boots, and woke my two companions.
We were wanted for thieving Government stock,
for each of us had escaped the hand of the tyrant
for the employ of a settler, for whom we thieved by night
from all the settlements. Our Judas had made a pact
with the police, jumping the fire with the two who hanged
while we went the other way into darkness.

I knew my way to the ends of the colony.
I had worked for Doctor Caley, while yet a boy
collecting insects: trap-door spiders and caterpillars
as thick as an index finger, covered with crimson hairs
that break off into your skin when touched, as sin does;
summer beetles which shine as though enchased with gold;
twigs which move without wind and resolve into limbs
and bodies, heads and feelers atwitch with knowledge of God.

I sat down by a large tree with the two untimely creatures
and remained there until morning. My joints then set
with cold, so that I could not rise without help.
We threaded the thick wood south, following a reedy stream
aslant with ribbons of eels and fulsome with crickets and frogs
towards Prospect where there lived a man I thought I could trust
with my life. I had no fear even though we were deathly cold
with shrivelled privates, our feet torn as if desiring thorns.

In a day and a night we made it to Luker's
but as soon as I entered his house I saw by his wry countenance
that he had a Judas heart and the Devil had locked his jaw.
But the Grand Arch Angel with flaming sword in hand
was guarding my poor sinful soul, and so his wife shifted him
off to Towngabby to see George Pell for clothing for us three.
She gave us a large cake of flour and a good piece of pork
as we lamented our horrid state, ruinous as wolves.

We set out once more for the house of Joshua Peck
through a dale of yellowed stumps like filed down teeth.
I made thanks to Merciful God who had brought us from the gulf of Hell
and delivered us from the tyrant, and snakes and wild beasts
that would devour a man. My companions tired of my preaching.
Soon we were at the house of Peck, who received us most efficaciously.
Mr Peck brought us some rags to cover our nakedness
and Mrs Peck told us that Luker had gone to inform on us.

We took our leave of these bright souls, and as Sister Peck had suggested,
we climbed the hill behind them, and from there saw Luker
and thirty untimely creatures dancing around the house of loving Peck
like the Serpent around the Garden of Job
when God permitted Job's temptation.
Then I arose and Farr asked where I was going.
I said I would go wherever the blessed Lord Jesus Christ pleased,
for as he brought the Children of Israel through the Wilderness

so the Redeemer would bring us through these sinuous and prickly woods.
We took the road to the Hawkesbury and travelled the night in silence.
We arrived at ten o'clock. Among the settlers Farr discovered one he knew
who said we could not stay, for the police and soldiers were expected.
I was given a cake and a piece of pork to carry,
but had only gone so far before my companions slipped away.
I was by myself. I went to the side of a large lagoon
where I lay down and grief overcame me. I thought my soul was melting.

I sought a sign from the Heavenly King, which would not be my first, nor last.
Eight years before when I lived with the Superintendent of Towngabby
I was watching his house at midnight when I saw my own person
stand before me, clear as clear, and say, 'so wonderful
shall all men be when they hear of the miracles
God shall work with you in this life.' At these words
I closed my eyes. When I opened them again, it was gone.
Cold sweat coursed through my hair and down my face in torrents.

This was my poor immortal soul leapt out of her chamber.
But now her seat was usurped by one of Satan's imps
so that on her return she had no place to rest, only bare walls
to cling to like a bat on a white sheet at night.
But a powerful angel that overlooks poor weak souls like mine
was passing and heard her pitiful cries, rebuked the evil spirit
and gave my soul her seat. This was the first of the signs
that proved a species of transportation. Nor am I free of these signs.

Even now in Greenwich as I relate this part of my life
three of the Beelzebub gang jump up in my room, demanding I go
with them to their master All three look like an old and tame baboon
I once saw playing with a child. When the child smacked it
on the head, the baboon would twinkle his eyes
and focus up his mouth as if sucking plums. Such are the faces
of these demons, filled with infernal lies by the Serpent,
which they soon vomit up, leaving me in peace.

Suddenly a body of geese, about six or seven thousand
appeared in the sky and descended so low I beheld them
perfectly white as snow. The lagoon was about three miles around
and these beautiful creatures covered one, making their circuit thrice
as if Jehovah had made a string fast to each and was playing with them
out of the window of Heaven. A whispering voice said,
'do not despair, behold the road thou art to take this day.'

In astonishment I saw the birds cluster in a shady place
then straight as a line they followed each other into the scarlet darkness.
I set out through the woods in the same direction as nigh as I could
and soon met a man who asked my business. I said I was gone
to banish myself from all society. Tears rolled down his cheeks.
I remained with him three weeks, during which time we learned of the hanging
of Farr and Meredith. Then I returned to my desert days
where it was ordained that I should wander in my transported state.

At last I met the man who preserved my life, good Gilberthorpe.
He took me to a large hollow tree at the back of his farm
where I remained some time. Each night I burned the trees off his land
until I cut my foot most dreadfully planting wheat in moonlight.
For fourteen days I remained where my friend had placed me
until my bandage fell off and my wound had closed
but I had lost the use of my right side. Good Gilberthorpe
brought his wife to see me, fearing that I would die.

I told them not to despair, that I would not die yet
by grace of the signs that God had shown me.
I told them of meeting my soul that time in Towngabby
and another sign shown me at dead of night
when the skies parted asunder and the light of heaven
was just like the light from a broken lamp
through the cracks of a door, shining no further
than where I lay. A voice said the Lord had heard my prayers,

that my life shall be recorded through all nations
and that those who hate me shall fear me. Then the heavens closed.
A third sign was in a dream where I fell down a steep hill
and came with great violence against an iron stanchion
which shook me so much I said that this was no dream.
There was a man by the side of these rails and I asked
what place this was. Under the rails there appeared to be a furnace
at full heat. 'This is Hell', he said, but yet no person was in it.

A fourth was a dream where I went to a house
with windows in the top of it, one of which was open,
and three Grand Angels were in the house, and three Goddesses.
I advanced to a glass case full of otherworldly jewels
and while I stood gazing, the Goddesses came to me,
and pointing to a gold crown covered with diamonds
the centre one said that this crown was for me.
I proceeded to a large table spread with something white

and the Goddess told me it was the canopy of heaven
and I must eat my belly full. And as I was eating
a beautiful man passed by the table, and the Goddess said
it was the Grand Arch Angel that brought the canopy
for me to eat. I watched him ascend through the window
at the top of the house and the Angels and Goddesses followed.
The next day Gilberthorpe came and laid me on the bole
of an old dead tree where I would be exposed to the sun

for the best part of the day, my lame side upmost.
Each night he came to remove me, repeating the same
until at the end of six weeks I recovered the use of my side
and began to walk again. For five months I remained with Gilberthorpe,
working at night and sleeping in daytime beside a beautiful stream
until the new Governor arrived, whose name was Philip Gidley King.
My friend Gilberthorpe went to him and told him of all my suffering
and how for five months he knew me to be hard at work.

The Governor straight away granted my pardon
and received me as if I had been one of his own children.
He was pleased to order me to New Zealand,
where I remained for seven months.
I lived there among the inhabitants, and consented
to be marked in the face when I received my wife.
She and my child have now been dead for years
and I have since grown used to the solitude of grief.

Chyort

Eye-deep in pollen I strode across the plain, cubed
by star pickets and their slack cross-hatchings,
sun-blind and sweating, the chunked city smoked
out of green fog, dodged traps and skirted trees brushing

a sky-powdered moon, sank ankle-deep in a dam's
dark border and witnessed the splashed rising of birds
and a frightened trotting of sheep, the spume
of silent aircraft knotted in thin white cords above,

heard the hiss of road trains braking, their savage
road-thundering, earth freshly ripped and steaming,
the sluggard river clay-bright and oozing
into cracked banks, stepped through a rust harvest

of doorless cars and a ripple of tattered barns,
through fields of scattered cardboard, bound
newspapers, slashed and slithery vinyl
chairs and a chipped glossy dog, tailless

and began to climb, fingernails dark rotting
crescents, up flesh-coloured sides thickly
reeking moist garbage, rasped knees
on sandstone polyhedrons and lodged boots squarely

under peeling roots and then rucked clear and strove
towards the mantle of sky scummed with cloud, dragged
back with each step in a skitter of fresh, pale rocks
and crabbed free, edging closer, ever as far.

From a Train in Connecticut

Petrillo's Used Auto Parts just outside New Haven
contains about a thousand newish cars
all wrecked, rusting, with tyreless wheels
and cataracted windscreens.
There's not a soul in sight, just the river
flowing slowly in mild lobes
swapping one bank for another.
In his office sits Joe Petrillo, worried about his weight
and listening to the radio, sweating
on the Mets getting back their stars
in time for the playoffs.

Centuries ago near what became New Haven
the Quinnipiac and the Pequot fought a series of battles
or skirmishes, really, the Quinnipiac coming off second best,
eventually selling their land to some Europeans
in exchange for a peace of sorts.
Nearby, firs serry up a hill, just as near Munich,
where not as long ago there was a similar appeasement.
It's hard to imagine. It seems so peaceful here,
although the creeping greenery is an intimation
of violence, full of life and humid intent.

Last night Joe dreamt he'd killed his oldest friend,
years ago, and had been getting away with it all this time.
Awake, he remembers that he has not seen him
for several years now, not since the friend moved
to Mystic, Connecticut. Or was that a mistake?
Perhaps there's blood on his hands after all.
He can't be sure, now, in the wide hours
of early morning, unbalanced accounts
before him in a yet to be ordered pile.

This is the problem, not his business or his weight
but that he never seems to coincide
with himself. Whenever he finds himself,
it's always provisional, like a ford
in a rising river. Most of all he is afraid.
The shuttered sun serrates the room.

The Potato

"One or the other of us will have to go,"
my father said, eyeing the last potato.
The last of its kind, for the moment, it sat on a plate,
the last of its kind, broken up from a deceased estate
scattered through antique shops and distant relatives
and patterned with its own objective correlative:
Koong Se walks behind the garden wall
worried about her imminent betrothal
to some Duke; meanwhile, her lover Chang
schemes to lure her into his Ford Mustang
or at least his dynasty's version of it: a souped-up Sampan
with modified oars and a comfy bridal suite. His flight plan
is simple enough: to an island where he and Koong Se will co-habit
and he will become famous for his writings. They will breed like rabbits.
What does Koong Se have to say about all this? She dreams
about Chang almost every night, of floating away downstream
and even though, the story goes, they elope,
she'd never leave her father or push the envelope
of filial piety, even if she had ever existed
instead of being part of some ham-fisted
chinoiserie from the land of intrepid explorers
and the agents of the potato's diasporas.
If it wasn't for the outbreak of potato blight
Ireland wouldn't have halved itself overnight
and my father's great-great-grandfather
wouldn't have come here with a brother
and two sisters who would scatter
to Mudgee, Berry, Parramatta,
Bathurst and beyond. There wouldn't have been me
playing with Mister Potato Head, somewhat pudgy
at three or four, plugging in a nose or an ear —
O where are the Mister Potato Heads of yesteryear?

Perhaps that's why it is the most human of vegetables:
we gouge its eyes out, stick it in the oven, then on a table
as I did later, serving my father his beloved potato.
Of course, he was the first to go.

Hospital

My deathbed has not yet been made
but has been manufactured
in a plant in Guangdong province

primarily by a man called Qing
who plays left halfback in the fourth grade
and is expert on the pressing machine.

We have common ancestors, Qing and I,
a man called Gan who lived in central Asia
and died in the year of the dog,

in the year of long rains and pestilence,
lying on a bed of camel-skin,
his fever abated somewhat by water

given him by my ancestor, Gan's daughter
who later married into the tribe of the red bear
then disappeared into the west

while Qing's ancestor, Gan's son
slaughtered a goat
and offered its blood to the wind god

and left its flesh to the elements,
having seen the good
that comes from tending to the dying.

3

Homecoming

Sun-damaged, sporty, wearing tracky-daks,
passengers can't be told from cabin crew
apart from their uniforms, their Australian chilliness;
        hedonists mostly,

serious adepts of physis, puritanical,
wary of alien cuisines, monolingual —
all of them start relaxing as cabin crew cross-check,
        landing gear lowers,

ailerons bristle, engines sough and earth climbs.
Longitude-trekkers. these new internationalists
humbled by nothing, not even their ignorance,
        chattering blithely,

wonder aloud how home has changed in their absence.
It hasn't, but they have. The world has reduced them to
miniature giants approaching a sparsely rich country,
        mulletocratic,

athlete-revering, distrustful of politics, obedient.
It's all about making money now, caring for investments as
if they were souls, or as if there was no such thing as a soul,
        or like, whatever.

Closer inspection, though, reveals great variety:
Shanghai-Chinese returning to investment properties;
Heibei tycoons, cashed up and itching to
        visit the casino;

taffy-haired surfers who get on at Cairns and stink of
wine-garlic night-before-breath; Euro-tanned
backpackers, double-chinned — even the fittest are
   Maillol-limbed beauties;

experts in security returning from Guangzhou to
Punchbowl; aromatherapists fresh from new franchises;
teachers of English and commerce students back for
   one more semester.

Where are the famous, the rich and powerful?
Prize-winning architects returning from Chengdu with the
Astrodome contract? Investment bankers from Stanmore?
   Fact-finding pollies?

Business or first class, economy, it doesn't matter:
pig-tailed professionals or t-shirted, unkempt and
scolding their children, they all speak the same
   vulgar-demotic.

Even the hosties are customers somewhere or other.
Difference is not really monetary — it's an asset. As
wheels kiss the tarmac, dawn strips them bare: so
   ugly they're beautiful.

Wire

Why're we
yeah nah
weird how we're all wireless now
worried hedonists
yeah nah
meaning: yes I'm worried, no I'm not a hedonist, or
yes I am a hedonist, and because of that I'm worried, or
yes I am a hedonist, and consequently I'm not worried, or
yes I hear you and it's fucked
yeah nah
word has it wireless is better than being wired
only some of us are wired
and we celebrate that with razors
yeah nah
meaning: yes it's true that we detain them
but it's not me who done it, or
yeah, the razors are sharp
nah, it's not a celebration, innit? Or
yeah they must be baddies
nah, only kidding, or
yeah, it's true
nah, my wireless isn't working here
too much inference
yeah nah
means, it's true, but I can't see it
means it isn't real
Innit?
yeah nah

Extinction

The two last speakers of the dying language
no longer talk to each other.

Oil: An Elegy

1.
It disappeared at the height of summer:
the highways were almost deserted
and the last sky-writing feathered into nothing.
Constipated clouds spat tiny drops
on smoking hills
and the hot winds ran on
across the deserts and bubbling roads,
baffling the cities and drubbing their glass scapes.

Hybrid cars misted the morning
and, smudge by smudge, smog disappeared.
Our lives shunted on. Hydrogen was farmed
from the sea, the wind yoked, sunlight harvested
and the boiling bowels of the earth went powering on;
but we had our last day as ourselves.

Now it is scattered through a billion skies;
the mantle of our dismantling;
but suburbia, which oil invented,
failed to mourn its passing, so busy
was the population waging war
on space and time. Then their words,
which had become so dense with oil and speed
discovered once more the air between them.

And in those days when the last rigs bloomed,
nostalgia ruled and all the motorists agreed
the day of its death was a major bummer.

2.

We went stupid on it: never where we wanted
to be, we used it up on fast-tracks to nowhere.
In the cities it gave us our daily bread.
It made possible the meeting of cornichons
with Incan woollens and Willy Wonka Bars.
It was the opposite of poetry:
oil made everything happen.
Now it lives on in the thermosphere
and flows through the pores of withered leaves
and lingers around the words of the living
like seas around bleached coral reefs;
poetry survived the incremental tide,
became a setting forth, thought's improvised canoe.

3.

Sky, receive our immolation —
the liquid states of the fossil nation;
receive into your greenhouse layers
the vanity of these, our prayers.

Waiting on Omotesando, Shibuya

Even here in Tokyo I emote the Sando
in summer: blue singlets and flannies,

cool enamelled walls which sweated
in the heat. Back then it all resolved

into a tonic: ecstasy and beer
crescending humidity. Outside

late arvo fell away down King Street,
a gathering mauve and solitude

which owned everything, even the music.
When it ended there was just the ringing dark,

a felafel roll for the walk home. Copious silence
drove the singling traffic. Nothing else.

Note: The Sando was the nickname for the Sandringham Hotel in Newtown, a popular music venue in the 1980s and 1990s.

The Man Who Loves Policemen

You've seen him at the footy or the Easter Show,
wherever there's a crowd and its controls: neither
like you nor himself, arms crossed, having a matey chat

with a couple of cops as if they were his brothers-in-law
at a barbecue, and not the law pumped up in leather
jackets, sunglasses, limp batons at the hip.

He loves these conversations: shooting from the lip
about the common Aussie yobbo, his habitat
and how to tame him. He talks with unselfconscious grace

as if bestowing membership to the human race
on his protectors, but the put-down passes: nothing rankles,
not even faded leg iron scars around their ankles.

Car Radio Shopping

Age means jazz in the ice
of your drink will not last
past the finger-breadth dregs,
will move on to the dirty hum
of traffic or a silk voice, announcing:

the ice in jazz means age
is a lever, a spring for the music
to gather the cool tones up
in exuberant flight, trailing
radio music from passenger windows,

means jazz age in the ice
of commerce, reducing hot buzz
to frozen desire, used car-yard
travesties, piped along the veins
of a fat city grid, under violet-white signs.

Jazz in the ice age means
songs of sadness and lava,
Martian ice caps photographed
by satellite, a dusting of fine red
paprika on cars parked in the street.

Curtains

Today there is a surfeit of light
and the curtains in the flat opposite
spread out of the window like an apron.

Two drunks, still going from last night,
dance slow dactylics on the street,
trying to hail a cab. Acorns of light

are planted everywhere
and invisible oaks rise up, spreading boughs
of heat. Traffic gnarls

and is combed out by the street.
Today is Sunday, a goat,
the day after Satyrday,

leaping from rock to rock
of the imagination, like surfing the net,
or surfing the light on a wave of heat.

Later, one curtain is blown back in,
exposing a black guitar case
and its clasp, a cool gleam.

Dams

1.
Kangaroos retreat into the dark needle-
floored pine forest.
Why do they always flee from us?
Because we know the answer already.

2.
Ochre lips prim
against the slouch of a hill.
Flat as the brim
of a shiny hat, the still
surface of the muddy dam.

3.
A dam surrounded by hoof-stamped mud
the colour of weak coffee:
a doubtful lip
pouts above the slope
holding everything in check.

4.
The dam, an old man's mouth,
sucking dryly.
A nymph has departed
its bark-hooked shell.

Everglades

Surging out of the past,
wave after wave of rock

crashes onto an estuary
of air. In the gully below,

daylight trickles through it
and a school of children blaze

without fear along its banks,
fuelling the sun's fire

with their shouts. Up past
the fenced stelography

of a scribbly gum
and its more recent graffiti,

they flash across the iron
fence posts on the pond's surface

in the bowed lip
of the stone wave still breaking.

Glamour

Sunset pinks the sportsman's bar
and dirty sweat glistens
like gold dust on their arms

as the drinkers listen
to the knowledgable drawl
of Smacker who, perched in a lipid sprawl

upon his stool, grades their conversation
with his steady tone, the master
of the stubble-scratch-and-frown,

a gesture he admired in Uncle Clem
and copied with apish diligence.
And by the others too — Smacker is their arbiter of elegance:

Dicko, for example, hawks his phlegm
and spits the way he's studied Smacker do it;
the way that Dicko rolls his sleeves

is copied by Chopper,
with the innovation of socks
at complementary half-mast,

now *de rigueur* for the lot.
How rich they seem in the gilding light:
the glittering, interlocking rings

left on the table by their drinks;
the lapidary condensation of their beers;
but richer still, the innocent ballet

of lumbering towards the bar,
a complicated dance whose artless steps
they've studied hard to master all these years.

Mountain Stream, Altiplano

The earth channels the sky
in a kind of sweaty trance:
inching furrows, shallow
finger-diggings of rain and dew

fork in jagged tines across the plateau —
and then the river wrinkles
into a blue scour so rapid
and flat it seems to be flowing uphill.

What's weirder is mountains shouldering
into the massively empty valley
and across them, dark lightning of dry stream-beds
striking upwards to the peaks.

The Lake

Words possess us
        with forgetfulness and love
makes us remember
        how to live: waking up
from dreams relieved
        the day does not flow
like the oneiric river

backwards up a hill,
        in one ear, out
another's, garbling
        onto the mirror
of the black lake
where every image

is a bullet from the future
        never seeming to break
the surface, a limited
indefinite remembering
the nothing beneath it,
        the black loveless nothing.

        That is the nightmare:
to dream of things
exactly as they are.

There was this lake. As clean as an eye but below its surface were sparse, slimy weeds. It was cold, much colder than the air and still as a pane of unbroken glass. It was the kind of place you went to to forget, only it was too shallow to let the past entirely disappear. Rowing out to the middle you found bits of yourself floating past, sinking slowly to the bottom or rising to the surface. Clouds were moving across the sky very quickly and their reflections were so big they almost capsized you. Still, you were happy enough: the entire world had become nothing more than the membrane upon which you drifted for what seemed like forever.

Notes

'The Narcolep': my mother, Elizabeth Anne Musgrave, née Quealy (1933-2016) suffered from narcolepsy and cataplexy for most of her adult life.

'Beijing Dectets': *qīngming* (清明), also known in English as tomb sweeping day, is a traditional Chinese festival which falls on the first day of the fifth solar term of the traditional Chinese calendar. This makes it the 15th day after the Spring Equinox, either the 4th or 5th of April in any given year. During *qīngming*, Chinese families visit the tombs of their ancestors to clean the gravesites, pray to their ancestors, and make ritual offerings, which typically include food and wine, the burning of joss sticks and hell banknotes, and the lighting of firecrackers.

gēge (哥哥), older brother.

báijiǔ (白酒), Chinese white wine.

sùsònghuà (宿松话) is the dialect spoken in Susong county, Anhui province.

'Waratah': George Thomas Ferris (1838-1903), the paternal grandfather of my paternal grandmother, resident in Waratah in 1866 at the time of his marriage. John Blake Quealy (1902-1978), great uncle who lived in Waratah in the 1930s. Dorothy Pawsey, née Downs (1791-1832), my 4th great-grandmother arrived in NSW in 1827 and died in Newcastle in 1832. Her daughter Eliza Augusta Prentice, née Pawsey (1822-1900), George Ferris's mother-in-law and my 3rd great-grandmother lived in and around Maitland all her adult life.

Moly-Cop: from its factory in Waratah, Moly-Cop manufactures the Comsteel product range of rail consumables.

Gryllus: the companion of Odysseus who refused to be returned to human form from that of a pig. See Plutarch's 'Beasts are

Rational' (Περὶ τοῦ τὰ ἄλογα λόγῳ χρῆσθαι — Bruta animalia ratione uti) from his *Moralia.*

京禧: 京 is the 'jīng' in Běijīng, meaning 'capital'. 禧 or 'xǐ' means auspiciousness, happiness or jubilation. 京禧 is a homophone of 惊喜, which means 'pleasantly surprised'.

'The Transportations of George Bruce' is adapted from two transcripts of the manuscript *Life of a Greenwich Pensioner 1776-1817*, one by Benedict Taylor and the other compiled by Thomas Whitley pre-1898. Grace Karskens refers to the Benedict Taylor transcript numerous times in *The Colony*, noting that 'Convicts were reported as working without clothes in the heat' (Allen & Unwin 2009); however, Bruce's story suggests that it was in winter that the raid took place on his gang. Although it may be that convicts worked without clothes at times in imitation of the Eora, Bruce's manuscript makes no mention at all of the indigenous inhabitants of the colony.

'Chyort': (чёрт) is the Russian word for 'devil'.

'Extinction': in 2011 this situation was reported with regard to the two last speakers of the language Ayapaneco in Mexico.

'The Potato': my father's great-great-grandfather Thomas Bernard L'Estrange (1819-1856): see my poem 'Death by Water 2' in *Phantom Limb* (2010).

'Oil: An Elegy' is written after Auden's 'In Memory of W.B. Yeats'

Acknowledgements

I am indebted to Greg McLaren and John Leonard for their close attention to the manuscript of this book, and would also like to thank Dael Allison, Judith Beveridge, Julie Chevalier, Charlotte Clutterbuck, Susan Hampton, Carol Jenkins, and Gail Nason of the Pomegranates for their helpful criticisms, as well as John Watson, Andy Kissane, Anthony Lawrence, Philip Salom, Todd Turner and Martin Langford for their edits and suggestions.

'Coastline' won the Newcastle Poetry Prize in 2012 and was first published in *Coastline: Newcastle Poetry Prize Anthology 2012* (Hunter Writers Centre 2012). 'Lines in Lviv, formerly Lvov, formerly Lemburg, near Limbo' was first published in *On First Looking*, edited by Jean Kent, David Musgrave and Carolyn Rickett (Puncher & Wattmann 2018). A version of 'The Project' was first published in *The Clambake: Cuplet 2018 Anthology*, edited by Claire Albrecht (Puncher & Wattmann 2018). 'The Narcolept' was first published in *The Australian* in 2018. 'Nine Crab Barn' was shortlisted for the Blake Poetry Prize in 2012. 'The Transportations of George Bruce' was first published in the Newcastle Poetry Prize Anthology 2016. 'Wire' was first published in *Writing to the Wire*, edited by Dan Disney and Kit Kelen (UWAP 2016). 'The Potato' and 'Fire' were first published in *A Way of Happening*, edited by Judith Beveridge and Carolyn Rickett (Puncher & Wattmann 2014). 'Hospital' was first published in *Best Australian Poems 2012* (Black Inc), edited by John Tranter. A version of *The Ash Field: 2. Naked* was first published in *The Canberra Times* in 2014. 'Homecoming' was first published in *Overland* (2011). 'From a Train in Connecticut' was first published in *Cordite* (2012) in English and in bahasa Indonesian.

www.ingramcontent.com/pod-product-compliance
Lightning Source LLC
Chambersburg PA
CBHW030855090426
42737CB00009B/1235